At the Zoo

Words by Eugene Booth
Pictures by Derek Collard

RAINTREE CHILDRENS BOOKS
Milwaukee • Toronto • Melbourne • London

Library of Congress Number: 77-7627

1 2 3 4 5 6 7 8 9 0 81 80 79 78 77

Printed and bound in the United States of America.

Library of Congress Cataloging in Publication Data

Booth, Eugene, 1940 —
     At the zoo.

     (A Raintree spotlight book)
     SUMMARY: Pictures of animals at the zoo stimulate
counting, identifying colors, "finding the mistake,"
noting visual differences, and other pre-reading ac-
tivities.
     [1. Zoo animals] I. Collard, Derek. II. Title.
PZ7.B6467At [E]   77-7627
ISBN 0-8393-0107-3 lib. bdg.

At the Zoo

Here is a zoo.
How many different animals can you see?
Which animals do you like best?

What are the animals and people doing?
What could happen next?
Turn the page and see.

Look back at the first picture.
What has changed?
Is this what you thought would happen?

If you could hear this picture,
what do you think it would sound like?
Make up a sound for each animal.

One, two, three, four.
Four, three, two, one.
Count the animals just for fun.

Zebras have stripes to help them hide.
See how many zebras you can find.

Which giraffe is little?
Which giraffe is big?
Which is the tallest and shortest tree?
Which trees can each giraffe eat from.

These penguins are playing in groups of
one, two, and three. Count each group.
How many penguins are there in all?

Look at the animals
on the tops of these pages.
Then look at the shapes below.

Which animal goes in each space?
Can you name each animal?

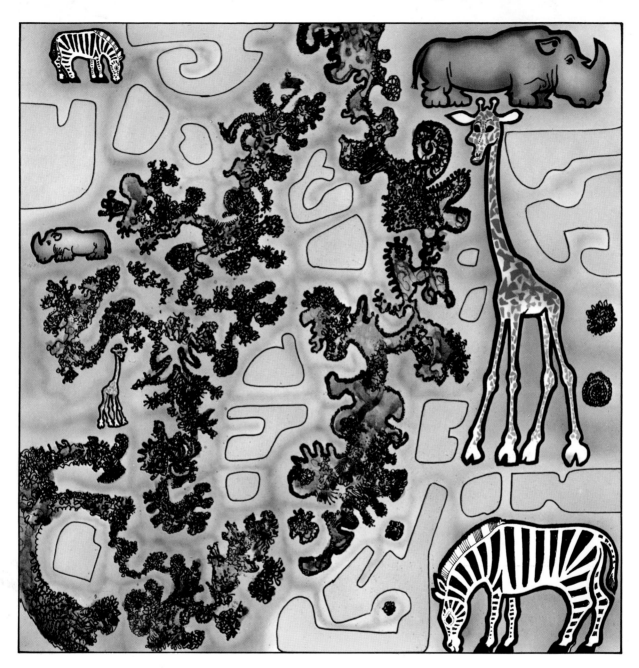

Here are three baby animals
that have lost their mothers.
Find a way for each baby animal
to go to its mother.

14

Here are three kinds of animals.
Can you name them?
Which animal in each group is different?
How many animals are there in all?

15

Count the animals in each group.
Which animals are big? Which ones are
little? Which ones have stripes?
Which animal does not go with its group?

These pictures tell a funny story about monkeys. Do you know what the story is? Talk about each picture.

Here is how the story ends.
What else could happen?
Where will the monkeys go next?

How many birds are in the cage? How
many are outside? What color is each bird?
How many birds are there of each color?

All kinds of things are wrong in this picture. Can you find the mistakes?

Make up a story to go with this picture.
What other funny things could happen
at this zoo?